The Angry Mom's Guide To Self- Regulation

A MIND-BODY APPROACH TO MANAGING YOUR EMOTIONS

Emilie Delworth

To all the mothers who struggle with dysregulation

CONTENTS

ACKNOWLEDGMENTS

I want to thank the many people who supported me and inspired me throughout my writing of this book.

First, my partner, Dave, for all the support and encouragement he has given me throughout our many years together. He has been a beacon of light for me as I've navigated my healing and overcome my issues with toxic anger. His support in furthering my education and writing this book means the world to me.

Next, my daughter, Lucy. She has given my life purpose in a way I have always craved. She challenges me, motivates me, and inspires me every day. She continues to gift me with showing me the parts of myself that I didn't know needed healing, and I am undoubtedly a better version of myself than ever before because of her.

I thank my lovely proofreaders, Hannah Reno and Dr. Melissa Reilly, and my Editor, Ally Arcuri. Their honest and encouraging feedback helped make this book what it is today.

And none of this would have been made possible without my former coach, Kat Kierans, for introducing me to the power of somatics.

Last but not least, I'd like to thank my many Instagram followers who inspire me every day to continue on my journey and share my process. Thank you for receiving my vulnerability with so much love and acceptance and helping me build the community we have built around @the.peaceful.mother. Thank you all for sharing your stories of healing with me. This book is for all of you, my fellow angry moms, who work hard to heal and break cycles.

INTRODUCTION

I wanted to be a mom my whole life. When I was finally blessed with the role of motherhood, my anger took me by surprise. I'll never forget the shame and guilt I felt, adding fuel to the fire of postpartum depression, anxiety, and rage that was burning inside me. "I'm a horrible mother." "I've made a terrible mistake." "I'm going to destroy her as my parents did to me" were just a few things I repeated to myself in those early months.

Can you relate? I'm guessing that since you're reading this book, you probably can. First things first - You are NOT a horrible mother, you have not made a terrible mistake in becoming a mother, and it's not too late to repair the hurt you may have caused your child.

At the root of every angry mom is a woman with unmet needs. A woman who is overwhelmed with stress, anxiety, and buried trauma. A woman who is disconnected from her body and conscious mind. This book is written for that woman - for you. I've designed this book to educate you and guide you through the same action steps I took to face my rage head-on. This book will guide you through reconnecting to your mind and body while helping you develop a personalized toolbox for decreasing your angry moments and practicing self-regulation when your anger begins to boil over.

I encourage you to invest in a journal, as this book includes many reflective journal prompts. If journals aren't for you, perhaps a Word document, voice memo system, or video diary is more your style. Find what works for you and commit yourself to doing the work at whatever pace is comfortable and sustainable for you. *Decide* that you *will* transform yourself through the teachings in this book.

Understand that healing and growth is often a process of two steps forward and one step back – give or take a few steps in either direction. Remember that the most sustainable changes are made slowly, and repetition is key for optimal results. You may need to read the same chapter, or even the same page, several times before it's integrated into your mind and the action steps have become habitual. I promise you that you will make mistakes along the way. I can also promise that months, even years from now, when you're transformed into the mom you have *decided* you will be, you will still make some mistakes. You will still take some steps backward sometimes. This is normal – it doesn't mean you're a failure. It means you're human.

As you embark on this journey of growth and healing, please remember that your child doesn't need a perfect mother. They need an accountable one. By reading this book, you're already on the right path.

ONE

BECOMING AWARE

The first step in learning to manage your anger is becoming aware. Becoming aware of what, you ask? Well, a few things - your emotions and how you experience those emotions, your triggers, your window of tolerance, and what stress response state/s you tend to default into. So, let's start by ensuring you're aware of all that even means!

EMOTIONS

Emotions are a mind-body experience. Mental states that are brought on by neurophysiological changes that typically elicit a behavioral response. Sometimes our thoughts trigger emotions, like when those pesky intrusive thoughts of bad things happening to our children suddenly creep in. Our hearts sink, our breath rates increase, and we immediately feel fear and despair. Other times, something experiential triggers the emotion, like when our friend sneaks up behind us and shouts, "Boo!" Our heart and breath rates increase, a wave of heat comes over us, and we immediately feel scared and maybe even angry. Regardless of what triggers our emotions, they exist within the body. The thoughts and beliefs we attach to them exist in the mind, but not so much the emotions themselves. At their core, I think of emotions as waves of energy.

So, if emotions are energy and energy doesn't die but rather flows, it stands to reason that when our emotions are suppressed, they can't flow through us and instead become stuck within the body. Pioneers in this type of research, such as Peter Levine, Ph.D., Dr. Gabor Mate, and Bessel van der Kolk, MD, have explored this phenomenon in depth, changing how we now understand trauma and stress, and disease.

PRIMARY EMOTIONS

There is much debate within the world of psychology as far as what exactly constitutes primary emotions. Some argue there are 5, some 6, 7, and 8. For simplicity's sake, I will go with the theory that there are five primary emotions – happy, sad, angry, hurt, and scared. The diagram below shows how all other secondary emotions are manifestations of these five basic emotions.

5 PRIMARY EMOTIONS

HAPPY	SAD	HURT/IN PAIN	ANGRY	SCARED
Excited	Disappointed	Grieving	Enraged	Terrified
Joyful	Hopeless	Heartbroken	Frustrated	Nervous
Grateful	Despair	Rejected	Annoyed	Worried
Silly	Sorrow	Betrayed	Bitter	Panicked

Whether or not we're aware, we're always experiencing emotions. We tend to think of emotions as negative or positive, but the reality is that emotions simply *are*. They're neutral. We assign the good or the bad to them, which is natural as our minds are designed to assign labels and fit concepts into boxes so that we may understand them better. We also do this so we don't waste our mental energy repeatedly processing the same concepts. Knowing that this is how our minds work and our bodies believe what the mind tells it, I prefer to shift my perspective on emotions to "pleasant" and "uncomfortable."

All emotions serve a purpose. Our very survival as a species is quite literally dependent on emotions. Emotions are messages from the brain, signaling whether things are potentially safe or dangerous. Anger, for example, is a signal from our body that something is physically or psychologically unsafe. As we know, anger can quickly turn from constructive to destructive, so let's take a closer look at what these two manifestations of anger might look like.

CONSTRUCTIVE ANGER

Constructive anger involves expressing your feelings and needs in a healthy, calm, respectful, and productive way. Constructive anger allows you to understand your circumstances better and the people you encounter, identify needs, and control situations. Constructive anger can lead to healing, growth, or learning.

For example, let's say my twelve-year-old is supposed to walk home from school every day, and I expect her home around 3:45 in the afternoon. On one particular day, the clock reads 4:05, and she still hasn't arrived home. I call her cell phone, and it goes straight to voicemail. Of course, I begin to worry, imagining all the worst things that could have happened to her. I think she's safe, but maybe she's succumbed to peer pressure to ditch home and go to the spot where all the "naughty" kids smoke weed after school. Maybe she doesn't care about our family's rules or how scared I must be. Another 10 minutes pass, the longest 10 minutes of my life, and she finally walks through the front door. "She's safe! Thank God!" I think before my mind begins assuming the worst of her, despite her always having been honest and responsible. My thoughts of her smoking weed must be why she's late. Rage boils over, and I want to yell at her, "Where have you been? You've had me worried sick! How dare you turn your phone off and come home late!"

Instead of yelling, I can recognize that my anger is simply trying to communicate a safety concern. I was scared that something terrible had happened to her and my body FELT it. My body didn't know what the threat was; it just knew something threatened it enough to activate my fight or flight response. Despite now knowing she's safe, my body is still holding on to those challenging emotions. My heart rate may still be high, I might still feel hot, and perhaps I begin to tremble.

After acknowledging my body's response, I take a moment to breathe as I hug my daughter. Despite still feeling angry, I can calmly express that I had been worried about her and was relieved she was okay. I can ask her where she's been and why she's late. She is then given the opportunity to tell me the story of witnessing a classmate hit a rock on her bike while riding home, which caused her to fly over the handlebars. The girl was all scraped up, her face bloodied, and she was crying hysterically. My daughter helped the girl sit up and called her mom to pick her up. It took a few calls to get ahold of her mom because she was at work, which is probably why my calls went straight to voicemail. She then sat and waited with the girl, so focused on keeping her calm and comfortable that she forgot to call me to tell me what was happening. Eventually, the girl's mom came to pick her up and offered her a ride home, but because my daughter had never met the woman, she felt it was safer to continue her walk home instead of accepting the ride. As she was processing the whole experience, she didn't think to call me while walking home. My daughter finishes her story with, "I'm really sorry I had you so worried, Mom. I was just so focused on helping. I didn't even think…."

Because I have been working on building the tools necessary to stay calm while expressing my feelings, I received the apology I needed. Because I could stay calm and direct in asking my daughter why she was late, I got the information I needed to move on from my anger and the stories I had attached to it. I could then explain to my daughter that I was proud of her for helping a classmate. I also request that she use this experience as a reminder to find the space to call or text me if anything like this happens again. At the end of this hypothetical situation, my daughter and I both had the space to be heard and could connect more deeply through the conflict.

DESTRUCTIVE ANGER

Destructive anger is the anger we "angry moms" are more familiar with. It involves expressing your anger in a harmful way, either to yourself or others, and is typically explosive and disproportionate to the circumstances. The harm caused may be verbal, psychological, or physical, leading to negative life consequences later and often a great deal of guilt and/or shame.

LOVE AND ATTACHMENT

Although love is far more complex than simply being a human emotion, I couldn't complete this section without discussing love and attachment. Love is more of a drive, like hunger, thirst, sexual arousal, etc. Humans *need* love to survive. We are pack animals by nature, and our bodies are designed to function more optimally when present and engaging in relationships with others. We need the loving connection of family, friends, community, and/or romantic partners.

Most importantly, we need a loving connection with our parent/s or primary caregiver/s. Our relationships with our primary caregivers lay the foundation for every other relationship we will ever have, including the relationship we will grow to have with ourselves. However, it isn't just a loving bond that human children need with their parent/s or caregiver/s.

Human infants and children need a secure attachment bond to their parent/s or caregiver/s.

The attachment bond between an infant and their primary caregiver (usually, but not always, their mother) is an emotional connection formed through subtle yet powerful nonverbal communication. It essentially wires into the infant's brain that their caregiver is good, reliable, and safe, that the infant is good and safe, and so is the world. The attachment bond that a child forms with their caregiver dictates the emotional and psychological health of the child for the rest of their life. The attachment bond is so critical that when given a choice between a surrogate mother made of metal that provided them with milk versus a surrogate mother made of soft blankets, the infant primates who were being studied notoriously chose the "mother" made of soft blankets, showing the high survival needs infants have for comfort. An infant or young child would quite literally die without the caregiver, so it is of vital importance that they attach to that caregiver.

The amazing thing about the attachment bond an infant forms with their primary caregiver is that it has little to do with how well-loved or cared for the infant is. It has far more to do with the nonverbal emotional communication developed between the infant and their primary caregiver. Nonverbal communication consists of facial expressions, gestures, posture, touch, tone of voice, and the pacing, timing, and intensity of speech, movement, or expressions. These subtle forms of communication have the power to make an infant or child either feel safe, secure, understood, and regulated - or not. As the child moves through childhood, their attachment to the primary caregiver may change, for better or worse, depending on how secure the caregiver manages to make the child feel in their emotions as they begin exploring their world. A secure attachment is formed when the child's emotional needs are met. When they are not, an insecure attachment is formed, typically leading to poorer long-term psychological, emotional, academic, and physical outcomes for the child and into adulthood.

The great news is that a child's attachment bond isn't set in stone, so even if potential signs of an insecure attachment are being seen in an infant or child - not meeting their developmental milestones, anxiety, avoidance, excessive fears, unwillingness to explore their environment and independence, low self-esteem, discomfort with affection or intimacy, suppression of emotions, or distrust of others - efforts made by their caregiver to make that child feel more safe, secure, understood and regulated can secure their insecure attachment bond. This is true for a child of any age, whether they're 2, 12, or older. The brain continues developing until our mid-20s and stays elastic and ever-changing for the duration of our entire lives, which means that it's never too late to start engaging in a more supportive emotional exchange with a child. The other piece of good news is that caregivers don't have to be perfect at being emotionally available to their children. No one can be perfectly attuned at all times, and everyone reaches their limit eventually. Fortunately, research shows us that ruptures to the attachment aren't just okay. They can be quite valuable when caregivers learn to repair those ruptures, big or small, by reconnecting with and reassuring the child that they're still safe, secure, and understood.

As I said, for those who grew up with an insecure attachment to their primary caregiver, poorer long-term outcomes are typically experienced. An adult with an insecure attachment style may have difficulty connecting with others, have a hard time feeling loved by others, feel anxious when their romantic partners are away, or have difficulty trusting anyone, among so many other possibilities. Learning about our attachment style can help us tremendously in understanding why we're prone to certain emotional triggers, the false beliefs we may hold that relate to those emotions, and why we react in the ways we do. Many of the mothers I have supported through their self-regulation journeys have wondered how they could have so many wounds to heal when they had amazing, loving parents and wonderful childhoods.

Attachment is, in many cases, the answer. Many of us had loving, nurturing parents. Still, because they hadn't been taught how to foster secure attachment, they may have unknowingly communicated a lack of safety, security, understanding, and calm to us, leading to insecure attachments. Chronically feeling unsafe and misunderstood *is* a form of trauma. Thankfully, as I previously mentioned, our brains are still quite elastic, regardless of age, and we can heal those wounds and shift our attachment styles as adults.

JOURNAL PROMPT – MAKING CONTACT WITH YOUR EMOTION WORDS

We know anger is a common primary feeling for you. Otherwise, you wouldn't be reading this book. I encourage you to take the next week to bring awareness to the other primary and secondary emotions you most frequently feel. As you identify these emotion words, write them down in your journal.

ACTION STEP – SOMATIC WITNESSING

As you catch yourself experiencing emotions, whether challenging or pleasant, take a moment to bring your awareness to where in your body you are experiencing each emotion. Don't try to fix or change them; witness them. Feel free to write about what you witness in your journal.

Where are you holding tension?

What parts of your body feel relaxed?

What temperature is associated with this emotion? Warm, hot, cold, or neutral?

Do you feel tingling, pain, numbness, or any other sensations?

TRIGGERS

A trigger is anything that starts a chain reaction of emotions within us, much like the trigger on a gun starts the process of the bullet being released from the gun's chamber. If the word "trigger" bothers you, perhaps replacing it with the word "activates" in your mind might work a little better for you. They are essentially the same. For the sake of consistency, I'll be using the word "trigger" throughout this book.

Triggers are emotional flashbacks to times when we were previously hurt. Regardless of how often we think about those painful experiences and whether we can even consciously remember them, our subconscious minds have held on to those experiences. Much of how we develop into the people we are today is influenced by these experiences.

For example, as a child, maybe my mom criticized me repeatedly, making me feel like I couldn't do anything right. So now, as I put special consideration into making my three-year-old daughter a lunch that I think she will eat, I am suddenly filled with anger when she shoves the food away and says, "Ew, gross. I don't like that." My anger may cause me to react with the typical behavior I am prone to when emotionally reactive — yelling. For some, it may be more like screaming, hitting, throwing things, etc. Essentially, in that sudden moment of anger, my daughter's response to her lunch triggered me to feel like I was six years old again, listening to my mother criticize the craft project I proudly brought home from school that day.

In these instances, we may become overwhelmed with the feeling that we can't do anything right. And with that, other associated emotions flood our bodies, triggering a stress response, otherwise known as a fight or flight response. This is all unconscious, of course. All we can easily identify in these moments is that our children's rude responses really piss us off.

The key thing to understand about triggers is that they have very little to do with the current event and much more to do with your past experiences. Yes, I may feel upset with my daughter for behaving in a way that I feel is rude, disrespectful, ungrateful, etc. But that is just the tip of the iceberg. Beneath my feelings about my daughter's very developmentally normal, yet challenging, behavior is the rest of the iceberg – the years of painful criticism from my mother, all of the emotions it elicited in me, and how it taught me to disconnect from my true self to receive her approval, and more importantly, preserve my attachment to her.

JOURNAL PROMPT – REFLECTING ON THE WEEK'S TRIGGERS

Think back on all the moments you felt angry this week, regardless of how you reacted to that anger. Answer these questions:

What was the event that triggered the anger? (e.g., My son climbed onto the counter after I told him not to).

What other emotions – primary or secondary – did you feel? What other associated feelings did you experience? (e.g., I felt frustrated that he didn't listen to my warning. I felt scared that he was going to get hurt. I felt out of control.)

What experience from the past might have been at the root of this current emotional reaction? (e.g., Watching my sister fall out of the tree and break her arm and feeling scared that she would die. I felt out of control as she fell and couldn't stop her.)

WINDOW OF TOLERANCE

The Window of Tolerance is a concept originally developed by Dr. Dan Siegel to describe a person's ideal arousal zone. The Window of Tolerance is the zone of optimal functioning, where individuals can effectively manage and cope with their emotions. In this zone, an individual is best capable of receiving, processing, and integrating information and/or stimuli. Outside of this zone, or "window," an individual might be functioning either in a state of hyper-arousal or hypo-arousal. Let's take a closer look at what each of these zones might look like.

HYPER-AROUSAL	WINDOW OF TOLERANCE	HYPO-AROUSAL
Speedy	Calm	Shut down
Impatient	Settled	Spacey
Aggressive	Grounded	Unable to focus
Angry/Enraged	Connected	Slow
Restless	Feels safe	Lethargic/Low energy
Impulsive	Able to think straight	Numb
Reactive	Steady heart rate	Withdrawn
Racing Thoughts	Steady respirations	Constipated
Anxious	Able to set boundaries	Lack of motivation or
Panicky	Able to be mindful	enthusiasm
Elevated heart rate &	Comfortable	Expresses little emotion
respiration	Engaged	Cold
Hot/Sweaty	Focused	Passive
Tight Muscles		Unable to focus

Windows of Tolerance come in varying sizes,
narrow, wide, and everywhere in between. Those
with more traumatic pasts and/or higher stress tend
to have more narrow Windows of Tolerance. It's
also important to note that an individual's window
will vary depending on different topics,
environments, and more. The good news is that the
width of our window is not set in stone. We can
widen our narrowed windows, and this book is
designed to help you do just that.

JOURNAL PROMPT – IDENTIFYING YOUR WINDOW OF TOLERANCE

Using the above table, identify which expressions of a "Window of Tolerance" apply to you. List any additional insights you recognize and indicate when you're functioning within your Window of Tolerance. (e.g., My baby's cries don't bother me.)

ACTION STEP – IDENTIFYING YOUR WINDOW OF TOLERANCE

For the next week, notice how often you're functioning within your Window of Tolerance. Would you say your Window is fairly narrow (not functioning within your Window very often) or fairly wide (functioning within your window often)?

HYPER-AROUSAL VS HYPO-AROUSAL

Hyper and hypo-arousal are essentially the stress states we experience when something triggers our "fight, flight, freeze" mode in the brain. We have our amygdala to thank for this, and as annoying as it can be, there are very important survival reasons why our amygdala constantly makes us feel so angry. The amygdala is responsible for regulating emotions, primarily fear and anger. It's also responsible for threat assessment and storing emotional memories. It was particularly important in the early days of human existence when we were never quite sure when a saber-toothed tiger would jump out at us. In the moment, the amygdala triggered a series of events that would prepare the human to fight or flee - the release of hormones, engaging certain parts of the body, and slowing down non-essential functions temporarily, like digesting food or even labor. Our amygdala would store the emotional memories and that of whatever environmental stimuli we experienced during close calls with such predators to ensure we were less likely to get ourselves into the same dangerous situations again, helping us survive.

We may not have to worry about saber-toothed tigers today, but our amygdala doesn't know that. The amygdala responds to a perceived threat, whether or not there is a legitimate threat to our safety. Whether we're watching a scary movie, getting yelled at by our parents, hearing our toddler scream in our face, or face to face with a lion, our amygdala perceives it all same and thus, fight, flight, freeze mode is engaged.

A few main factors can influence how narrow our Window of Tolerance might be and, thus, how frequently we're functioning from a state of either hyper or hypo-arousal. Hyper-arousal is the state we're in during fight or flight mode, and hypo-arousal is when we're in freeze mode. These states are a state of dysregulation, the very thing we're working to address in this book, and we are learning to self-regulate when dysregulated.

The first factor is how much trauma or how many stressful events we experienced in our past, especially during childhood. Remember that trauma is how we *perceive* or *internalize* an event, not the event itself. Trauma can certainly be experiencing abuse or some other "big T trauma," or it can be how you *internalized* constantly being told to stop crying, being put on time-out a lot, feeling abandoned or rejected and never understanding why, or some other "little t trauma." Another factor is the type of attachment we had to our primary caregivers – secure or insecure. And last but not least, how much, if at all, our caregivers modeled and taught us emotional regulation.

JOURNAL PROMPT – IDENTIFYING YOUR STATE OF DYSREGULATION

Using the table above, add up how many stress reactions in both hyper and hypo-arousal you frequently experience. Which state of dysregulation are you more prone to, or are they equal?

ACTION STEP – AUTOPILOT EXERCISE

What does your autopilot look like? Using the table above, write down which stress reactions you frequently experience. Add any other reactions you might recognize.

TWO

WHAT LEADS US TO SNAP

Now that you have a better understanding of what you're feeling and the stress states you tend to default into, let's delve deeper into why you keep snapping, despite how badly you want to stop.

Knowledge is great, but it doesn't do us much good if we can't couple it with action. We can know something like the back of our hands. Still, when we find ourselves flooded with uncomfortable emotions, that knowledge goes right out the window, and we default to the same behaviors we know are inappropriate. Let's explore the various factors that lead us to continue making the same mistakes repeatedly, no matter how many times we promise ourselves (and our kids) it won't happen again.

FACTOR 1: THE WOUNDED INNER CHILD

"Inner child" has become quite a buzzword in today's society, and rightfully so because it is a powerful and useful concept that allows for deeper levels of self-analysis and healing than previously imagined. The term inner child refers to the aspect of our subconscious mind that develops from our experiences in our formative years, from birth to about 12 years old. What's less talked about are the other "family members" we carry within our psyches, including the inner teenager and the inner critical parent. These parts of the psyche can be thought of as an aspect of your character that can often take over when faced with a challenge. Understanding our inner child can bring tremendous results like discovering and releasing repressed emotions, resolving dysfunctional patterns of thought and behavior, better recognizing unmet needs, increasing self-worth and self-care, and so much more.

THE HEALTHY INNER CHILD

The healthy inner child encompasses the emotions and parts of our personality that were nurtured in the ways we needed as a child. The healthy inner child feels safe, seen, heard, confident, comfortable, and loved.

THE WOUNDED INNER CHILD

The wounded inner child results from how our subconscious was programmed in response to not getting the nurturing we needed. It encompasses any emotions or parts of our personality that were suppressed in childhood. We *all* have a wounded inner child, no matter how amazing our childhood was. This is a tough one for many people to accept, but it's true. None of us had perfect parents, even if they were incredible parents, and none of us had perfect teachers, friends, or lives free of adversity.

Then there is the intergenerational trauma that we inherit on an environmental level. If our parents were regularly told to "stop crying" and taught to suppress their emotions, they likely parented us in the only way they knew how – the way their parents parented them. Then we, too, were taught to suppress our emotions through repeatedly being told to "stop crying." This may not seem like a trauma, but it is. And it is chronic. As I previously mentioned, trauma is not the events that occur but how we internalize the events. When we experience a stressful event as a child, big or small, and are supported and nurtured through it, it's less likely to be a trauma for us. However, when we experience a stressful event as a child, big or small, and are *not* supported or nurtured through it in the ways we need, it's likely to become a trauma for us.

Finally, we inherit intergenerational trauma on a cellular level. Think about it. Eggs are formed in a female's body when she is a fetus in her mother's womb. This means that everything our mother went through when she was pregnant with us and everything our grandmother went through when she was pregnant with our mother is engrained in our DNA. Along with everything our great-grandmother experienced while pregnant with our grandmother. Thanks to the discovery of epigenetics, we now know that the DNA we inherit is not written in stone. We *can* change our DNA. We can rewire our brains and ultimately change our life's outcome through mental and behavioral practices.

When we're triggered, it is the wounded inner child that is being triggered. The wounded inner child is experiencing the emotional flashback to trauma from when we were a child. Recall the example in Chapter One of my critical mother and the experience of being triggered into an emotional flashback over my daughter not wanting the lunch I made her. It is the inner child that suddenly feels like she is right back in that painful moment, and she has no idea if we are grown up now or if it's just a memory. To the inner child, the fear, shame, and pain are just as real now as they were back then.

THE MISGUIDED TEENAGER

The misguided teenager is the version of the inner child that has grown up a bit. When the wounded inner child gets triggered, if the healthy inner parent isn't present to respond, the teenager sometimes shows up to try and protect the inner child. Because the teenager is misguided, their attempts at protecting the inner child involve destructive behaviors that ultimately only hurt the inner child more. The inner teenager lashes out, gets aggressive, and engages in dangerous situations because it gives them a false sense of power.

When we react to being triggered with what I refer to as "adult temper tantrums," it is the inner teenager. When we lash out with aggression in response to being triggered, it is our inner teenager.

Many of our false beliefs are rooted in our inner teenagers. The misguided teenager tells us we were fools to think that person actually loved us. The misguided teenager tells us not to get too excited about our progress or blessings because we're only going to end up failing again – or life will find a way to screw us like it always does. Believe it or not, this is the inner teenager's misguided way of trying to protect the inner child – of trying to protect *you*. She doesn't know you're all grown up now. How could she if the healthy inner parent doesn't show up when the wounded inner child is triggered?

THE HEALTHY INNER PARENT

The healthy inner parent is a parent who accomplishes their primary role of protecting, nurturing, and guiding their child or children. The healthy inner parent can regulate their emotions, consistently respond to their child with patience and compassion, and upholds whatever boundaries are needed to keep the child safe and healthy. When we get triggered but can take a moment to breathe and regulate, it is the healthy inner parent that is responding.

THE TOXIC INNER PARENT

The toxic inner parent is either a parent who is not present, leaving the inner child to fend for themselves, leading the inner teenager to feel like they need to step up. A toxic inner parent is also a parent who is emotionally unavailable, abusive, critical, and/or inappropriate. The toxic inner parent fails to uphold boundaries and verbally abuses the inner child. The inner teenager lashes out to hurt others, but the inner toxic parent lashes in to hurt *you*.

When we become triggered and default into aggressive reactions, the wounded inner child is triggered. But, it is either the misguided teenager or the toxic inner parent who reacts with destructive and/or abusive behavior.

REPARENTING THE WOUNDED INNER CHILD

"Reparenting" is the practice of giving ourselves the nurturing and protection we didn't receive in childhood. Identifying what our wounds are can be a helpful first step, but as I stated before, it's not necessary to remember our traumatic experiences, nor is it necessary to go into the process of reparenting knowing what our specific wounds are.

Many different exercises can help us connect with and reparent our inner child. For those who experienced a particularly traumatic childhood, it is recommended to go that route. Still, it's also important to note that we're reparenting ourselves each time we grow as individuals. Each time we replace our critical inner voice (that pesky mom guilt) with compassionate statements, we're reparenting ourselves. Each time we choose to care for ourselves in some way, we're reparenting ourselves. Each time we're able to respond to our child with nurturing and respect in ways that we didn't experience as children, we're reparenting ourselves. So, as you learn to self-regulate more, you will ultimately be reparenting yourself at the same time.

JOURNAL PROMPT – WRITE A LETTER TO YOUR INNER CHILD

When you have the time and feel safe, take a minute to close your eyes (if it feels comfortable for you) and imagine yourself at the age of five in your mind. See her. Hear her. Witness her personality. Observe her emotions.

Now write your five-year-old self (your inner child) a letter. What does she need to hear? Need to know? Does she need an apology? Does she need to know she's worthy? Does she need guidance? Validation? Don't overthink it; write what's on your heart.

FACTOR 2: AMYGDALA HIJACKING

As you now know, we have our amygdala to thank for our angry outbursts. Typically, after the fight, flight, or freeze mode is triggered, the frontal lobes will step in, bringing rational, conscious responses to the forefront, overriding the amygdala. Surviving the threat of a saber-toothed tiger is obviously important, but so is our ability to get back to daily life by finding food and shelter, eating, sleeping, having sex, etc. The frontal lobes know to step in once the threat is eliminated to return to other aspects of survival and procreation.

However, when particularly strong feelings of anxiety, fear, or anger are experienced in response to a stressful situation, the amygdala will sometimes override the frontal lobes, leading to explosive, aggressive overreactions. Let's explore what this might look like in one of the more commonly triggering situations we mothers face – tantrums.

A sensory stimulus is perceived; your young child is screaming. Your auditory nerve picks up the soundwave generated by your child's screaming. It converts it into an electrical impulse that travels to the thalamus, which relays sensory signals. Then it moves onto the amygdala before reaching your prefrontal cortex, which oversees your logic and thinking. Before you even have a chance to logically process the loud screaming, let alone identify where it's coming from (your innocent child), your amygdala has already begun preparing your body for a perceived threat, tensing your muscles, increasing your heart rate, and so on. Before you can even process what's happening, you're yelling at your child to stop.

Other common examples of amygdala hijacking include when a car cuts you off while driving, leading you to become so enraged that you scream at them and flip them off. Another example is when your partner says something that makes you angry, and you throw the plate you're holding at them. Or potentially, when your friend is telling you a story as you watch your child almost fall from the top of the playground and you're in such a panic, you don't hear anything your friend said.

BUT WHY?

"Okay, but *why* is my amygdala hijacking my brain?"

The more our brain perceives threats, the more conditioned it becomes to engage our threat or stress response system. For those of us living in the modern world, inundated with constant stressors, in a society more debilitated by anxiety disorders than ever, we become more prone to amygdala hijacking.

This hijacking is even more ingrained in us if we have a particularly traumatic past.

When we're children, and sometimes even as adults, we're faced with situations that send us into a stress response, but because we're small and mostly helpless, we can't fight or flee. Let's say I'm six years old and my alcoholic father has come home raging drunk again. He is angry and has me backed into a corner, screaming at me. Naturally, my fight-or-flight response is activated, but I'm just a tiny 6-year-old, so there is no way I can fight him. I also depend on him to feed me and keep a roof over my head, so I can't just run away from the danger. I now have two options. I can fawn, try to behave in a way that pleases him, or freeze by shutting down and/or submitting. Instinctually, I know that nothing I have done thus far has pleased him, so my best chance at survival in this scenario is to freeze or shut down. Much like an antelope, whom a tiger has just snatched up, instinctually knows its best chance at survival is to play dead. If the antelope plays dead, which is ultimately a result of its body shutting down while its brain remains in a hyper-aroused state, the tiger is more likely to hide the antelope somewhere while it retrieves its cubs for dinner. In that time, the antelope can escape its freeze state and run away to safety, thus completing the stress response cycle. The problem we humans face is that we have somehow become disconnected from our innate ability to complete these stress responses. As a 6-year-old girl constantly facing potentially harmful or deadly violent situations in the home, I may have learned to freeze or shut down in stressful situations. But, I maybe *didn't* learn how to bring myself out of it, resulting in trauma.

That unfinished stress, or trauma, stays stuck in the body until it's finally completed, which in today's day most often means never. Unconsciously, my body spends the rest of my life crying out for a chance to complete that stress response cycle. I unconsciously seek out men just like my father in an attempt to relive and finally complete that stress response. I don't complete it, though, because I don't know how, and I don't even realize that's what I need. More trauma becomes trapped in my body over time, I become more and more prone to overreactions, and my amygdala becomes more and more prone to hijacking my logical brain.

Now I'm a mom, full of unresolved trauma, faced with tantrums, and an uncooperative child. My brain hears her scream, "No!" at me and perceives this scream as if it were a tiger about to attack. My instinct to counterattack is activated through my fight or flight response, which is felt and expressed as rage. Since I am an adult now, I *can* attempt to fight back, and it feels like every fiber of my being wants to fight because of my compulsion to complete that stress cycle I've been holding onto for so long. In reality, not *every* fiber of my being wants to attack. My frontal lobes know what my amygdala doesn't, which is that I'm not face-to-face with a tiger but rather with a small, helpless child — *my* precious, helpless child.

The good news is that we *can* stop this hijacking by inviting our logical brains back online in those pivotal moments with awareness and practice. We can even learn to prevent future hijackings.

JOURNAL PROMPT – REFLECTION

Think back on the past week and write about any situation you can recall when you experienced amygdala hijacking. Remember that this is any situation where you went from calm to suddenly and intensely emotionally reactive. Your body may have started shaking or sweating, you may have become nauseous and tense, and you may have experienced rapid breathing or heart rate. Answer these questions:

How many times did you experience amygdala hijacking this past week?

What emotions did you experience during the hijacking?

What symptoms did your body experience?

What, if any, were the most common triggers for you?

FACTOR 3: UNMET NEEDS

It can be incredibly difficult to identify our needs as a mother, let alone meet them when we have a crying baby in our arms and a whiny toddler at our feet. Not to mention the phone that won't stop ringing and our partner who wants to know when dinner will be ready. Meanwhile, we haven't sipped water all day, skipped lunch, forgot to brush our teeth that morning, our back aches, and we haven't had a moment alone in five days. Can anyone really blame us for eventually snapping?

Society lectures us about the importance of self-care with no guidance on how to *do* it when you're being pulled in a million different directions. "It takes a village," they say, and we're all looking around, wondering where that village is. Our society is more disconnected than ever, and mothers feel crippling pressure to "do it all" – an expectation that no human can meet. "Sleep when the baby sleeps," they tell us, but who will do the laundry, the vacuuming, the cooking, the scheduling, the organizing, or caring for the older children? Who will *do it all* while we're resting and rejuvenating?

With each new child we bring into the world, or welcome into our family through adoption, we are reborn into a new mother. With that often comes an identity crisis. Whether we work or stay home, we question who we are, aside from "Mommy" now. How are we supposed to even know what we need now? What are we worth other than being our family's caregiver? And with it comes guilt that we aren't good enough or perfect enough at being pulled in all these different directions. Resentment builds, we grow exhausted, and before we know it, snapping at our families has become our default mode.

It doesn't have to be this way, though, I promise. As challenging as it can be to identify and meet our own needs, self-care doesn't have to be that complicated. If the term "self-care" bothers you, let's start by shifting our perspective around it. What resonates most with you? Self-love? Filling your cup? Refueling your love tank? I will use "self-love" from here on out, but feel free to replace it with whatever terminology works best for you.

Self-love looks different for each of us. When most of us think of self-love, we think of bubble baths, spa days, or girls' nights. Maybe we think of a workout, a hike, or a backpacking trip with girlfriends. But self-love can also be letting your kids watch a show while you read a chapter out of your book. It can be listening to an inspiring podcast or audiobook with one earbud in while you cook dinner, turning on your favorite song and having a dance party with your kids, or letting the laundry pile wait so you can take a few moments to journal and practice your self-regulation tools. Self-love can also be asking for help when we're drowning under the pressure to do it all.

Self-love can also feel overwhelming and inaccessible to many of us because we think we need a lot of time to tend to our needs and desires, but it doesn't have to take a bunch of extra time. As I said in my previous paragraph, self-love can be practiced *with* your kids, as is the case with the dance party idea, and it can be practiced *while* tending to your responsibilities, as with listening to a podcast while cooking. Much of my self-love practicing has also happened while nursing my daughter or contact napping. I've used that time to meditate, journal, practice self-regulation exercises, read, write this book, etc.

Now that we've established how to meet our needs amidst our busy lives, let's take a deeper look into what our needs might be.

SURVIVAL/HEALTH NEEDS

Survival needs are obvious. They consist of eating, hydrating, getting adequate sleep (easier said than done as a mom, I know), using the toilet, and ensuring a safe environment. Our physical health needs go a little deeper in that they aren't needed to survive the day or week, but they are needed to truly thrive in life. Health needs consist of limiting what, in my family, we call "red light foods," otherwise known as junk food, and eating enough nutritious foods, or "green light foods." Plus, we need to ensure we get enough activity or movement in our day, take supplements or medications, and tend to our hygiene.

EMOTIONAL/PSYCHOLOGICAL NEEDS

Emotional needs include creating the space to check in with our inner worlds and feel, process, and release our emotions. Psychological needs consist of ensuring that we feel heard, seen, validated, respected, and safe. This also includes anything that makes us feel stimulated, joyous, and grateful, such as learning new things, viewing beautiful scenery, listening to beautiful music, feeling inspired, feeling connected to others, and so much more.

JOURNAL PROMPT: TAKING INVENTORY

How often do you get your survival/health needs met within any given day?

What are the hurdles that make meeting those needs challenging?

Can you think of any solutions to those hurdles?

List five opportunities throughout the day when you can take 2-5 minutes to meet those needs better.

Now, how often do you get your emotional/psychological needs met within any given day?

List five different ways your psychological needs tank gets filled.

Now, list five daily opportunities when you can take 2-5 minutes to better meet your emotional or psychological needs.

FACTOR 4: LACKING SKILLS

EMOTIONAL INTELLIGENCE

Emotional intelligence is a fairly new phenomenon. The term was originally coined in 1990 when researchers began recognizing the importance of understanding one's emotions and learning to process and regulate them. Of course, "emotional intelligence" didn't become more widely used and understood until recent years. This means that emotional intelligence was likely not something our parents were aware of as we were being raised in the 80s or 90s. It was not commonplace to pause and check in with one's emotions, let alone healthily process them or regulate them. Instead, our parents knew to react to their emotions rather than respond more intentionally. They were taught to blame their emotions and reactive behaviors on us, their children, and our challenging yet likely developmentally normal behaviors. Our parents didn't grow up in a world where acknowledging past trauma and working to reprogram past conditionings was the standard. Not much was known about trauma until recently.

With this lack of knowledge and, thus, skills, our parents were left to parent by default. They were left to carry on the same patterns passed down from generations before them or, at best, attempt to break cycles with little to no resources for healing their wounds or parenting in alignment with scientific evidence.

Children learn best through what is modeled for them, and if we didn't have emotional regulation modeled for us, how can we be expected to go into motherhood with these skills? Unless, of course, we happen to have entered motherhood while already studying such psychological matters. I am guessing you didn't, just as I hadn't.

Not only did we not have emotional intelligence modeled for us, but we also didn't have somatic intelligence modeled for us because it's a new phenomenon. You may even be asking yourself, "Wait...What in the heck is somatic intelligence?"

SOMATIC INTELLIGENCE

"Somatic" is a word that is ultimately used in reference to, or regarding, the body. "Somatic intelligence" refers to the awareness and understanding of the body, its processes and sensations, and the ability to release trapped energy, emotions, or trauma. This is important because, if you recall from Chapter One, emotions *are* a neurophysiological reaction in the body. Whether the emotion is pleasant or uncomfortable, our body is driving our experience of it, at least at first. We get "butterflies" in our bellies when we're excited, and our heart rates increase when we're scared.

Reconnecting with our bodies is important for our physical health. Few of us take the time to truly connect with our bodies, and why would we when it's not something we're taught to do? How often have you heard of a man dying from a heart attack with supposedly no prior symptoms? Or a woman who had no idea she was pregnant until she was giving birth? Their bodies spoke to them; they didn't know how to listen. Reconnecting to our body is also vital if we are to develop the skill of emotional intelligence, and to do that, we must also develop the skill of mindfulness.

MINDFULNESS

Amazingly, neuroscientist Jill Bolte Taylor discovered that our physiological experience of emotions only lasts 90 seconds in the body. Hard to believe, right? When our toddler is on their fifth morning tantrum, and our patience is officially tapped out, our anger sticks around for much longer than a minute and a half. And why is this? Because of the stories, our minds begin telling us about the experience. "Oh God, not again! I swear she's *trying* to piss me off at this point! She's clearly trying to manipulate me!" Of course, who wouldn't be mad with a line of thinking like that? Nobody likes to be manipulated. But is it true? I can guarantee it isn't. The toddler's brain is far more developed in the emotional part and not so much in the logical, rational part. Tantrums are a manifestation of brain development. Through these tantrums and our ability to co-regulate with them, they learn emotional intelligence, resulting in the ability to regulate their emotions in healthier ways.

Mindset shifts are another skill that few of us had modeled for us. We tend to come up with a thought or elaborate story and automatically believe it. Through practicing mindfulness, we can recognize these stories for what they are and replace them with more objective truths or, at the very least, more loving thoughts.

CAUTION: Be aware of toxic positivity! Toxic positivity is a dysfunctional approach to managing emotions that attempts to ignore any emotions deemed "negative" or, as I prefer to call them, "uncomfortable." Its toxic message is spread through common phrases like "Positive vibes only." "Get over it!" and "Just be positive!" It's also commonly experienced by those grieving or dealing with mental health disorders. "At least they're in a better place now." "You just have to focus on gratitude!" These are all well-meaning phrases that allude to the likelihood that those speaking them have unconsciously been taught to suppress their uncomfortable emotions or who have been taught that uncomfortable emotions are bad, unsafe, or unacceptable.

Don't get me wrong, positive thinking has its place, as does gratitude. The key is to find the balance between feeling and honoring your challenging emotions, accepting your pain and life's hardships while not becoming trapped there, but rather being able to release those emotions and manage the stories our minds tell about those feelings and experiences. Sounds hard, right? Of course, because, again, few of us had this modeled for us as children. It takes practice, but the good news is that the brain is quite elastic and capable of great changes with enough repetitive practice.

ACTION STEP: BODY SCAN – Video tutorial available at www.the-peaceful-mother/book-tutorials

[Note: Please ensure that you are in a location where you feel safe when you do this. If you are new to connecting with your body, you may wish to have a trusted friend/partner or a pet present.]

Begin by finding a comfortable seated position. Close your eyes if it feels safe.

Take a deep, grounding breath through your nose and release it slowly through your mouth. Feel your bottom on your seat. Take another breath in and release as you feel yourself sinking deeper into your seat, held, safe.

Now bring your attention to your head. Notice any sensations you may feel. Do you notice warmth? Cold? Pressure? Pain? Tingling? Try not to judge what you feel, nor change it. Just witness it.

Next, bring your attention to your face. Notice any sensations you may feel. Are your eyes tired? Are your ears clogged? Maybe a little flyaway hair is tickling your forehead. Just witness what you feel. Notice whether the sensations are uncomfortable, pleasant, or neutral.

Continue down through your whole body, taking the time to notice what is in each section of your body. Your neck, your shoulders, your chest, your arms, your hands and fingers, your back, your belly, your hips, your legs, your feet, and your toes. Notice where your body meets the back of your chair, if applicable. Notice how your seat feels against your body. Is it hard, soft, fuzzy, or itchy? Are you holding tension anywhere?

Next, bring your awareness to your heart rate. Is your heart beating fast or regularly? Lastly, bring your awareness back to your breath. Witness your breath for as long as feels safe for you.

Take one last grounding deep breath in through your nose, and slowly release it out through your mouth. Take your time coming back. Wiggle your fingers and toes, rotate your head in circles, and slowly begin moving your body as you open your eyes and return to your environment.

JOURNAL PROMPT: REFLECTION

How was that experience for you? Write about anything that felt significant for you.

THREE

BUILDING YOUR TOOLBOX

Video tutorials can be found at
www.the-peaceful-mother.com/book-tutorials

Hopefully, by now, you're beginning to understand the source of your anger more deeply and the factors that lead it to boil over. These next few chapters are where you really begin to learn how to shift from reactive to proactive. In this chapter, you will learn your first action steps in making this transformative shift. As I've previously said, knowledge is an important step in the process of learning to manage your anger, but without action steps, knowledge doesn't do you much good. It's important to learn how to regulate your nervous system so that you boil over less often and can more quickly regain control when it does happen. The exercises I share in this chapter will both help you begin widening your window of tolerance *and* become more capable of overriding that amygdala hijacking when it does occur, inviting the frontal lobes back into the driver's seat of your experiences and allowing you to make more conscious choices in how you respond to life's challenges.

It's important that you practice doing these exercises often, regardless of how you feel. As I mentioned in the introduction, the brain learns through repetition, so practice these for a few minutes every day, or at the very least, most days. If you can create the space to practice for more than just a few minutes in a day, even better! Think about when your child has learned new skills – rolling over, crawling, walking, riding a bike, etc. How many times did they try and fail before they finally mastered the skill? A lot, right? This process will look the same for you. You will forget to practice some days. You will practice diligently when you're calm, and then you'll get triggered and completely forget to self-regulate in the moment, falling into your same default angry reactions. But in time, the more you practice, your body will begin to remember these new skills. Your brain will integrate this new knowledge and understanding with these new skills. You'll find yourself slowly becoming triggered less often and begin remembering to regulate before snapping more often.

Before we get started, let's go over the number one challenge most mothers, particularly if they have young children, face when presented with the task of practicing these self-regulation exercises, or any self-love activities, for that matter... Time to practice!

FINDING SPACE TO PRACTICE

Begin by setting small goals for yourself. As I've stated before, the most sustainable goals are made slowly. If you currently don't make space for any self-love activities, you may want to start with a goal of practicing these techniques 2-3 days a week and work up from there. If you're a little more accustomed to making time for yourself but are still working with a jam-packed schedule, you may want to start with 3-5 days a week and work up to every day from there. In either case, you may want to start with just 2-3 minutes daily and work up to 5-10 minutes a day or more. Again, take it slowly when working your way up to increased sessions and time frames. Set small new goals. If it's not working out for you, return to where you were, or decrease your increase slightly. There is no shame in going back.

Find what is practical for you. I promise you will find results with even a couple minutes a few times a week if that's all that's realistic for you.

Write about each new goal in your journal. The more detail, the better. Writing our goals down in detail helps our brains remember our goals better. It also helps to have a physical container for our goals that we can re-read and review regularly. I find it especially helpful to post new goals and perspective shifts around the house, car, or office, where I regularly see them. And again, repetition is how our brains learn best, so the more we write our clear goals down, the more quickly our minds can integrate the intention and remember to practice.

Create a schedule for yourself and set reminders on your phone. Schedule in your calendar or write in your journal the time slots you intend to practice. Be careful not to attach yourself to these slots. Life happens. Our children skip naps, stay home sick from school, and many other things may come up. If you forget or skip a session, aim to make up for it another day or time, if possible. If not, remind yourself that you're doing your best and give yourself grace.

If scheduling time slots doesn't work for you, find the little pockets of time throughout your day where there are lulls. Your children are playing independently, napping, watching TV, or perhaps you set them up with an activity. Much of my practice had initially occurred while my daughter nursed or contact napped on me. I've even practiced while in the shower or using the toilet. Ideally, our children are either not around or being fully entertained by a movie or activity, but since this is not always possible, find what pockets of time feel accessible and safe for you.

Once you feel safer connecting with your body, you can involve your children if you're new to this type of work. I began practicing with my daughter when she was two years old, and she loved it. It was fun for us to connect, and I often made it silly when I could. She made up her own affirmations to recite while tapping, my favorite being, "I am dog, and I am frog." The shaking and sound release made her laugh. Practicing with children should always be child-led. If they aren't interested in practicing with you, don't force it. Even if your child is playing next to you while you practice a quick exercise, you are reaping the benefits and modeling for them what self-love and regulation look like.

PRACTICING SELF-REGULATION

I highly recommend that you take your time with this chapter. Repeat each exercise a few times before you begin trying the next one. Check in with yourself before each exercise by testing your nervous system. I will explain how to do this in the next section of this chapter. Testing your nervous system will allow you to truly identify which of the regulation techniques in this book are right for you, and which aren't. During each exercise, check in with yourself mentally. Ask yourself, "How does this exercise make my body feel? And my mind? Is this exercise working for me?" After each exercise, test your nervous system again.

If any of these exercises induces or increases anxiety or pain in you, please stop. *Listen* to your body. Your body is your guide. Sensations are positive, distress is not. If practicing these exercises begins to fill you with any emotions that are too intense to process on your own, please seek the support of a therapist or somatic practitioner in your area.

The purpose of this chapter, and this book, is to guide you in developing your *personalized* toolbox. You might walk away with only a few of the tools offered here. No matter how your toolbox is filled in the end, it's exactly the right toolbox for you. You may try the exercises that don't work for you later. They may feel more appropriate once you've connected more deeply to your body, widened your Window of Tolerance, and attained a more regulated nervous system. There was a time when I couldn't focus on my breath without triggering anxiety and feeling like I was going to suffocate. In time, I gained the ability to focus on my breath without any issues, and now breathwork is a huge part of my practice.

If connecting with your body is something completely new to you, it's also not a bad idea to practice these in the presence of someone you trust - a partner, a close friend, or even a pet. You want to ensure that you feel safe in your environment and can focus your full attention on these exercises so that you may feel safe journeying into your inner world.

Now, let's get started, shall we?

TESTING

Testing our nervous system allows us to have concrete evidence of whether we're in a dysregulated state or not. Dysregulation tends to be clear when we're noticeably emotional, but often the signs that we're functioning outside of our window of tolerance are subtle, and, therefore, difficult for many of us to recognize given how disconnected from our bodies we have grown in the years since our infancy. Testing our nervous system before a regulation exercise gives us a baseline. Testing after a regulation exercise allows us to identify whether that exercise worked to regulate us, didn't do much for us, or perhaps pushed us further into a dysregulated state. This feedback from the body empowers us in knowing when we may need to adjust our approach, and which exercises should be excluded from our toolbox.

I have included three options for testing because, as with regulation exercises, not all tests are effective for every person. For those with hypermobility, the first option may be your best bet.

NECK ROTATION

Begin with your head facing forward. Turn your head as far as it will go to the right. Take a mental note of how far you're able to rotate in this direction. Next, turn your head to the left. Take a mental note of how far you're able to rotate in this direction. It may help to find a focal point in front of you on each side, to help you remember how far you were able to go.

Test again after each regulation exercise and notice whether you were able to rotate further than your baseline test, about the same, or not as far.

TOUCHING TOES

In a standing position, bend at the waist and touch your toes, or the ground, or as far as you can go. Keep your legs straight, with just a slight bend at the knees to avoid hyperextension. Take a mental note of how far you're able to touch down.

Test again after each regulation exercise and notice whether you were able to bend further than your baseline test, about the same, or not as far.

TRUNK ROTATION

In a standing position, extend your arms out in front of you, clasping your hands together, with your thumbs pointing upward and your index fingers pointing forward, as if to form a gun with your hands. Keeping your legs straight and facing forward, rotate your torso at the waist, to the right. Take a mental note of where your fingers are pointing. Next, turn your torso to the left. Again, take mental note of where your fingers are pointing.

Test again after each regulation exercise and notice whether you were able to rotate further than your baseline test, about the same, or not as far.

CONTAINMENT

As I've previously discussed, our emotions are neurophysiological experiences, meaning they reside within the brain and the body. As Peter Levine, Ph.D. explains in his book, Healing Trauma, our body is the container for these neurophysiological experiences and the boundary that separates us from other people and our environment. He explains that when we become wounded by our traumas, however big or small, that boundary gets ruptured, leaving us feeling raw or unprotected. This containment exercise, adapted from an exercise provided in his book, is designed to begin repairing that rupture to your boundary, allowing you to feel safer in your body and more wholly you.

Take your time with this exercise. It may take a while but connecting with your body, your container, in a way that allows you to truly feel and take ownership of it is important in becoming somatically intelligent and more capable of self-regulation.

TAPPING EXERCISE

Find a comfortable seat. Notice the parts of your body that are making contact with your seat – your bottom on the floor, your back against the pillow behind you, your arms and hands on the chair arms, etc. Notice how each of your body parts feels against the objects they are contacting.

Next, gently tap the palm of your left hand with the fingers on your right hand. Continue tapping on your left hand for as long as you need to gain a sense of that body part. Once you have a sense of your hand, stop tapping and take a moment to reflect on what you're sensing. What do you feel in your hand? Heat, tingling, numbness, etc. While looking at your hand, say, "This is my hand. My hand is a part of me. My hand belongs to me."

Next, turn your hand over and tap on the back of your left hand. Repeat tapping as long as you need, stopping, then stating, "This is my hand. My hand is a part of me. My hand belongs to me."

Continue this process with your right hand, then the rest of your body. Include your forearms, your upper arms, your shoulders, your chest, your belly, your hips, your butt, your thighs, your lower legs, your feet, the top of your head, your face, and your neck.

ANCHORING & GROUNDING

An anchor, often referred to as "grounding," is a mental image or sensation that serves as an anchoring force in bringing us back to our mind-body when engaging in mindfulness or somatic practices. When you notice your mind wandering away from this present moment, an anchor serves to bring you back to your mind in the *here and now*. When you feel emotionally activated, an anchor, or grounding, brings you back into your body in the present moment. Whatever you prefer to call it, anchoring or grounding acts as a reminder that you are safe in your body and this space, right here and right now. If you begin to feel lost as you move through the exercises in this chapter, use these anchoring or grounding techniques to bring you back to yourself.

I'll give you a few options. You choose what serves you most.

SELF-HUG

Take your right hand and cup the left side of your torso, just under your armpit. Next, take your left hand and cup your right arm under the shoulder. Breathe. Check in with how this feels for you. Continue for as long as you feel you need to.

VISUALIZATION

Close your eyes if it feels safe. If it doesn't, focus your gaze on a point in front of you. Imagine the image of a long, thick, strong rope with an anchor attached to the end. Imagine that this rope is attached to the core of your body. Breathe. Once this image is clear in your mind, take a deep breath in, and on your exhale, imagine that this anchor, attached to this long, thick, strong rope attached to your core, descends through the ground, through the layers of the earth, into the core of the earth. Imagine your anchor sinking into the core of the earth. One end of the rope is attached to your body's core, the other to the earth's core, anchoring you into this space, into the here and the now - safe. Breathe. Once this image is clear, begin wiggling your fingers, then your toes, open your eyes, and return to your environment.

SOMATIC GROUNDING

Close your eyes if it feels safe. Bring your attention to your seat – your chair, the floor, the grass, whatever it is that your bottom is making contact with. Notice how your bottom feels against your seat. Take a deep inhale through your nose, and feel your bottom settle deeper into your seat on your exhale. Next, bring your attention to any other parts of your body that are in contact with your seat –

your back against the chair, your legs on the rug, etc. Notice how it feels in your body to be in connection with your seat. Breathe and feel yourself being held in this space.

REGULATION EXERCISES

While the exercises previously shared in this chapter can certainly be effective tools for regulating the nervous system (i.e., your emotions). The following exercises will provide various options to choose from to fill your toolbox with both activating and calming exercises for when you're hypo or hyper-aroused. Inspired by a yogic breathwork concept coined by Lucas Rockwood, I have divided the exercises into Water, Whiskey, and Coffee.

As much as I recommend trying all the exercises at least once if they're safe for your health status, I recommend starting with the ones that align most closely with your more natural expressions of anger. If yelling is your challenge, the sound-releasing exercises may be a good place to start. If hitting or spanking is your challenge, the shaking or more physical exercises may be a good place to start.

Remember to check in with yourself before, during, and after each exercise, and refer to my instructions at the beginning of this chapter.

WATER EXERCISES

Water, as we all know, is good for us. No matter what we're doing or feeling, water is beneficial for us. The same goes for these exercises. These are balancing exercises that can be done regardless of what state you're in. These are great go-to exercises that won't throw you out of your Window of Tolerance and into an aroused state if done under the wrong circumstances.

BALANCED BREATHING

Find a comfortable seated or standing position. Close your eyes if it feels safe. Bring your awareness to your breath for a moment. Don't try to change it yet. Observe.

Next, take a deep inhale through your nose for a count of four, then immediately release it through your mouth for a count of four. Repeat this exercise as many times as you need to.

EFT TAPPING

Find a comfortable seated or standing position. Close your eyes if it feels safe.

Begin by establishing a setup statement by stating what's bothering you and rating your distress on a scale of 1-10. Then come up with a statement of acceptance. For example, "I am feeling angry with my son's behavior. My level of anger is an 8. I am allowed to feel angry."

Begin the tapping sequence by tapping your fingers along your meridian points. Seven to nine taps of the top of your head, your forehead, the top of your cheekbones, just below and to the side of your eyes, your upper lip, your chin, your chest, your sides, just below your armpits and towards the back, and the side of your hand, between your wrist and pinky finger. As you tap along your meridian points, voice your feeling of distress, followed by a statement of acceptance. For example, "Even though I feel angry, I know I am allowed to feel angry."

Rate your level of distress on a scale of 1-10 again. Continue the sequence as many times as you need to feel regulated.

MERIDIAN TAPPING

Begin by using your fingers to tap along your meridian points. Seven to nine taps on the top of your head, your forehead, the top of your cheekbones, just below and to the side of your eyes, your upper lip, your chin, your chest, your sides, just below your armpits and towards the back, and the side of your hand, between your wrist and pinky finger.

You may follow along the meridian line or choose a spot that works best for you. Two common spots for isolated meridian tapping are the chest and the sides of the hands.

CUPPING

With your hand in a cupping position, begin by tapping your opposite side shoulder. Tap with your cupped hand 5-8 times, then continue down your arm, taking your time with each section of your arm. Next, tap your other shoulder and continue down that arm. Continue tapping your whole body, using your cupped hand, for as long as you need to feel calm.

Alternatively, you can gently squeeze each section of your body with your cupped hand rather than tapping.

VOO BREATH

Begin by taking a deep breath in through your nose. As you exhale through your mouth, say, "Voooooo." This sound should come from your throat, expressed as a deep "Voo," eliciting a feeling of vibration in your throat. Breathe for a few moments and repeat as needed.

SOUND RELEASE

Growl, hum, sing, scream, moan – release sound in whatever feels natural. Stick with one sound or alternate between a few. Do this as long as you need to feel calmer.

BUTTERFLY HUG

Close your eyes if it feels safe for you. Cross your arms across your chest, resting your open hands at the base of your shoulders, covering your armpit area. Gently tap your hands against your body, one at a time, as if your hands are butterfly wings. Notice how your fingers feel as they contact your body. Notice how your body feels as it connects with your fingers. Breathe and flutter your butterfly's wings three times on each side, or longer if you need.

TENSE & RELAX

Begin by clenching your hands into tight fists. Hold it for 5 seconds and then release, relaxing your hand muscles. Breathe. Move through the different areas of your body, focusing on the parts where you feel tension. Clench your muscles for 5 seconds and then release. Breathe. Repeat each body part once more, if desired.

Alternatively, you can squeeze a ball or pillow or sit in a chair and press your feet against the ground as hard as possible. Hold for 5 seconds and release, relaxing your muscles.

JAW MASSAGE

Gently massage the jaw area of your face with your fingertips. Massage around your chin, up towards your cheeks, and towards your ears. Massage as long as you need to feel calm.

SOOTHING TOUCH

Begin by lightly running your fingertips on your right hand along the top of your left hand and down your fingers. Continue slowly up your arm. Breathe. Pay attention to how this feels on your skin. Next, lightly run your left fingertips along the top of your right hand and down your fingers. Continue up your left arm. Breathe. Continue running your fingertips lightly and slowly along any or all of your body parts for as long as you need.

SENSORY STIMULATION

Option 1 - Run your hands under cold water for a few moments. Bring your awareness to how the water feels on your skin and nails. Then switch to warm water for a few moments and notice how that feels on your skin and nails. Alternate for as long as you need to feel calm.

Option 2 – Take an ice pack or a package of frozen veggies from the freezer and place it against the skin on the back of your neck. Breathe. Remove the ice pack after 10 seconds, maximum, to avoid giving yourself a cold burn. Next, place the ice pack against the skin on your upper chest. Breathe. Remove after 5-10 seconds. Alternate between the back of your neck and your chest as much as you need to feel calm.

INNER CHILD VALIDATION

Close your eyes if it feels safe. Place your right hand on your chest and your left hand on your tummy. Breathe. Imagine yourself as a little girl at whatever age comes to mind first. Imagine her feeling the distressed emotion that you're feeling in the moment. Now, either aloud or in your mind, validate her feelings. For example, "It's safe to feel angry. You're allowed to feel angry. Anyone would feel angry about this. You're safe. I've got you."

If it feels right for you, imagine that you're giving your inner little girl a comforting hug. Breathe. When you're ready, open your eyes.

WHISKEY EXERCISES

Whiskey is a fine beverage in moderation, but too much of it will easily throw a person off. Whiskey is also famous for putting people to sleep. These exercises are valuable for *calming* the nervous system, but they should be done in moderation and should largely be reserved for when one is hyper-aroused to avoid being pushed into a state of hypo-arousal.

BOX BREATHING

Find a comfortable seated or standing position. Close your eyes if it feels comfortable for you. Bring your awareness to your breath. Don't try to change it yet; just observe.

Next, inhale through your nose for a count of four, then hold your breath for a count of four. Try not to inhale or exhale. Just hold it. Then, exhale through your mouth for a count of four. Repeat this exercise a couple more times, or as many times as you need to feel calm.

LONG EXHALE BREATHING

Find a comfortable seated or standing position. Close your eyes if it feels safe. Bring your awareness to your breath. Don't try to change it yet. Just observe.

Next, take a deep inhale through your nose for a count of four and then release it through your mouth for a count of eight or until your breath is fully emptied. Repeat this exercise three to ten more times, depending on your needs.

VAGUS NERVE MASSAGE

This exercise may be done with both sides at once or just one side at a time, depending on what is more accessible for you.

Begin by placing your index and middle fingers of each hand on your neck, just below your ear lobes. Begin slowly, gently massaging your neck in an up-and-down motion, only moving your fingers about an inch or two down your neck, then back up. Breathe. Massage for 30 seconds to a minute. Check in with yourself and continue for another short session as needed.

EAR MASSAGE

This exercise may be done with both sides at once or just one side at a time, depending on what is more accessible for you.

Begin by forming a "C" with your index finger and thumb. Now, place your index finger at the lower end of the opening of the inside of your ear. Close your "C" into a ring by placing your thumb behind your ear. Slowly massage your ears by moving your ring in a circular motion forwards four times. Now move your ring in a circular motion backward four times. Repeat once more.

ARCH FLUCTUATION

Begin by standing with your legs hip-width apart. Breathe. On your next inhale, while keeping your feet flat on the ground and your legs straight, imagine that you're pushing the arches of your feet down into ground. On your exhale, imagine that you're pulling your arches back up, away from the ground. Your movements should be subtle. This is largely done in the mind, intending, or willing our arches through these subtle movements.

YAWN

Begin by opening your mouth wide as if to yawn. Move your jaw around a bit as you keep your mouth open. This will likely initiate a real yawn for you. You can pretend to yawn if a real yawn is not initiated. Make the sound, feel the sensation, and move your mouth as you would during a yawn. Feel your body releasing any tension or stress as you push your breath out and close your mouth, ending your yawn.

COFFEE EXERCISES

Coffee is another beverage that is fine in moderation, but too much of it will lead to jitters, insomnia, anxiety, and other undesirable side effects. These exercises are valuable for activating the nervous system but should be used in moderation. Specifically, they should largely be reserved for when one is in a hypo-aroused state to avoid being pushed into a state of hyperarousal.

SHAKING/TREMORING

Begin by gently shaking your hands for about 15 seconds. Slowly begin integrating more of your body. Shake your arms, wiggle your torso, shake your legs and feet, and shake your head. If it feels safe for you, slowly begin shaking a bit harder. If a harder shake doesn't feel right for you, you may do a more subtle tremor, as if you are shivering from the cold. Shake or tremor for 1-2 minutes, then slowly begin to settle your body again.

Once you've come to a stop, breathe, and check in with how you're feeling. If it feels right for you, begin the process of shaking/tremoring again and continue for up to two minutes.

If this is your first time doing this exercise, stop after two repetitions. As you practice this more regularly, you may repeat this exercise up to five times, as needed, checking in with yourself between sessions.

BREATH OF FIRE

This breathing exercise focuses on the exhale and not the inhale. Begin by pushing your breath out through your mouth in quick, short spurts. Continue your exhales one right after the other, 15 times. Each should last about a second.

You will naturally breathe in between each exhale, but it is not where your focus should be. Your focus is on the rhythm of each one-second exhale.

If this is your first time doing this exercise, limit your time to 15 seconds. As you begin practicing this more regularly, you can slowly increase your time by five seconds each session until you reach a minute. Do not exceed one minute.

FOUR

FINDING THE PAUSE

Now that you've begun to build your toolbox of self-regulation techniques and have created more of a habit around practicing these techniques, we will be moving more deeply into your level of awareness around your triggers. The key to this process is to create enough space between the feelings being triggered in you and the action you follow up with – finding "the pause." Typically, for those with narrow Windows of Tolerance who are more prone to amygdala hijacking, there is a very tiny space between our being triggered and the action we take. That is if there's any space at all. For some, it may feel like you're reacting before you can even register your anger or process what just happened to illicit that anger in you. For others, you may recognize that you're triggered, and you may even recognize the true source of the emotion (the experience you're re-experiencing on an emotional level). Still, you probably don't yet know *how* to stop yourself from behaving in hurtful ways that you later regret. You'll learn about the "how" in the next few chapters. But first, let's ensure you've learned how to lengthen your pause enough so that the *how* is even attainable. Awareness is key here, and increasing awareness comes in three phases.

PHASE 1 – REFLECTING AFTER THE FACT

This is the phase where a lot of angry moms get stuck. It's a vicious cycle of getting triggered, being reactive, and then feeling guilt and shame-ridden, beating oneself up over the reactive behavior. For many, the remorse stage of the cycle involves promising oneself that it'll never happen again, only to become overpowered, yet again, by their emotions, and then the compulsive behavior to react in destructive ways. Sound familiar? You're not alone in that, I assure you!

The first step in shifting out of this vicious cycle is recognizing your remorse's value. The fact that you recognize the dysfunction in your reactive behavior, and the guilt you feel over it, means that you've already taken your first step in raising your awareness. Think about it: how many times did you hear your parents apologize when they snapped at you? Many, if not most, parents walk (or perhaps stumble) through parenthood, unaware of how destructive their reactivity is for their children. This doesn't make them bad parents; it just makes them unaware. Celebrate the fact that you are already one step closer to breaking that cycle for your family!

Now for the real work.

The next time you find yourself in the remorse stage, aware that you had been triggered and reacted poorly, take a few minutes or more to reflect on it, and write about it in your journal. This can happen right when you realize the error in your ways, or you might have to wait until just before bed. When you write out your reflections doesn't matter as long as your reflections are taking place within 24 hours or so of your experience or experiences.

JOURNAL PROMPT: REFLECTION

Reflect on the last time you were triggered and got reactive. What emotions were you feeling? Anger, yes. Anything else?

Now write about any underlying feelings you can identify. For example, feeling unsafe, out of control, or disrespected may be at the core of your anger.

If you can remember an experience or series of experiences that might be where these feelings are rooted, great! Write about it. If you don't have many childhood memories or aren't sure yet, no problem. This is a bonus step, not a necessary one.

Next, reflect on how you felt in your body when you were triggered. Were you hot or cold? Did you feel tension anywhere? Were you clenching your fists or your jaw? Was your heart racing? How was your breath rate? List everything you notice.

Now, write about your ideal response to this scenario for next time. Be careful to avoid getting too attached to this ideal. It will take time and practice before you respond with intention rather than unconsciously reacting. This is to get your mind visualizing alternate, healthy possibilities.

ACTION STEP: SOMATIC RELEASE

Now that you have brought your awareness to your body's experience of your emotions in that heated moment, take a moment to release some of that energy that may still be stuck in your body. Take a few deep breaths in through your nose and exhale them fully through your mouth. As you breathe, imagine that you are releasing any emotional residue from your body and state, "I release all anger [insert any additional emotions felt] from my body." Relax your body a little more with each exhale.

PHASE 2 – CATCHING YOURSELF IN THE MOMENT

The next phase in the vicious "angry mom cycle" is being able to actually recognize that you're triggered and reactive *in* the heat of the moment. For some, catching yourself mid-reactivity is enough for you to shift your behavior immediately. This is where scripts like, "I don't like how I just reacted. Let's have a do-over," can be used. However, awareness isn't enough for many individuals who struggle with anger to override reactive behavior.

I recall times when it felt like I was watching myself scream at my daughter from outside my body, thinking, "This isn't okay. She's a child. She's behaving completely understandably, given her stage of development. I'm scaring her. I need to get ahold of myself." And yet, I couldn't figure out how to stop screaming or yelling in that moment. It was almost as if I was watching someone else in control of my body. In a sense, I *was* watching someone else in control of my body, my inner misguided teenager, attempting to protect my wounded inner child who had just had those old wounds triggered.

Graduating from this place of being completely overpowered to the next phase was a slow progression. Eventually, I was able to stop myself from screaming or yelling. Because I didn't yet have access to any alternative form of release, I would still stomp around huffing and puffing or speaking to my daughter in a very mean tone, blaming her for my feelings and behavior, quickly bouncing between expressions of remorse and then anger again. This is when I really knew I needed to learn a healthier way to release the fiery energy that was burning through my veins, and I set out to learn all I could about somatics. Once I began practicing the somatic self-regulation techniques I share in this book, I was propelled forward in my journey through the "angry mom" cycle. My hope in writing this book is that you will not have to suffer through this maddening stage nearly as long as I did.

When I use the word "maddening" to describe this phase, I truly mean it. Nothing makes you feel crazier than being completely out of control of your body and behavior, especially as you mentally will yourself to stop – unsuccessfully. It's terrifying to be so out of control of your body; it triggers your wounded inner child in powerful ways. This phase may elicit guilt and shame in you to a degree you haven't yet experienced. That is your inner child. This phase may make you feel like a failure– that's your inner child. Trust me, you aren't a failure, and you aren't crazy. You're reading this book! You're doing the work and on your way to becoming the more regulated version of yourself that you aspire to be. Connecting with your inner child and giving her the love, acceptance, and encouragement she needs is the key to releasing guilt and shame.

Think of this phase like a transforming butterfly. The caterpillar doesn't just form a little cocoon case around herself to become a butterfly. She must *become* a chrysalis, literally morphing her body into a new, even more vulnerable, form. She shakes as her body uncomfortably morphs into a new version of herself. In time, that vulnerable new form, the chrysalis, cracks open to release yet another new version, the beautiful butterfly with wings to soar to new heights. This is the chrysalis phase of your transformation. It's uncomfortable. It might even be scary. But I promise you that through this process, you will be able to transform into a new mother and a new woman with wings to soar to new heights.

JOURNAL PROMPT: REFLECTION

Take a moment to reflect on your earlier experience of catching yourself in the heat of the moment. Write about how that scene unfolded for you.

Were you able to regulate yourself and have a do-over once you caught yourself?

Were you unable to stop yourself from reacting in a dysfunctional way, despite being aware of how destructive it was?

What emotions and underlying feelings did your experience elicit in you? For example, maybe you felt scared because you were out of control. Or maybe you felt angry with yourself for being a "failure."

Next, reflect on how you felt in your body when you were triggered. Were you hot or cold? Did you feel tension anywhere? Were you clenching your fists or your jaw? Was your heart racing? How was your breath rate? List everything you notice.

Next, identify contributing factors that may have made you more vulnerable to snapping. Were you hungry or dehydrated? Were you tired? Have you made space for enough self-love practice today/this week?

Lastly, reflect on what you can learn from this experience. How can you better care for yourself throughout the day and in the moment when faced with these overpowering emotions?

ACTION STEP: REPARENTING YOUR INNER CHILD – Video tutorial available at www.the-peaceful-mother.com/book-tutorials

Close your eyes if it feels safe. Breathe. Imagine yourself in an all-white room. As you look around at the white walls, you notice a child sitting on the corner floor across the room from you. She's curled up, her arms wrapped around her knees, her face at her knees. You see her shaking slightly, and you realize she's crying.

You slowly walk over to her and introduce yourself. You ask her if it's okay that you sit with her. She nods yes, so you sit across from her. You ask her why she's crying, and she responds, "I'm such a failure. Everything is my fault. I'm a bad girl." She sobs harder.

You extend your arm and gently rest your hand on her shoulder. "Is it okay if I hold you?" you ask. She nods yes through her tears, so you scoop her into your lap and bring her close. At first, you let her cry as you rock her, stroke her hair, or maybe softly rub her back. After a few moments, her cries get quieter, and she's left trembling in your arms.

You look down at her sweet, wet eyes and tell her, "I see you, and I love you exactly as you are. None of this is your fault. You don't have to hold onto this pain and this pressure any longer. You're safe with me. You can let it go now."

You watch as her little face looks up at you, and you see her sad, wet eyes give way to an innocent sparkle. She nods that she understands. She's ready to release her shame and her guilt. You hug her for a moment and then ask if she'd like to stay in your magical heart pocket with you. She lights up, excitedly nodding yes.

With your next inhale, you watch as she shrinks down, small enough to fit in the palm of your hand. With your next exhale, you gently place your inner child into the pocket of your heart. She is safe with you. She is you. Breathe.

When you're ready, begin slowly moving your fingers and toes. Gently move your head from side to side. Open your eyes and return to the world.

PHASE 3 – CATCHING YOURSELF BEFORE REACTING

This is the phase where the pause is found. Here, you have learned to catch yourself being triggered and possibly tempted to react in the same destructive ways you're used to, but you have enough awareness now to create a gap between the moment you're triggered and the action you take next. Rather than *reacting* emotionally, that gap provides you enough space to *respond* consciously.

Of course, this likely won't happen every time you're triggered, not even the most seasoned "conscious parents" nail this process perfectly every time. We *all* hit our limits sometimes, so we all make mistakes. The key is for those mistakes to be the minority and for us to repair any ruptures they caused afterward. I encourage you to aim for the 80/20 rule. If 80% of the time you can regulate yourself and respond rather than react, and only 20% of the time you are being overpowered by your emotions and getting reactive, you're nailing it! The ultimate goal should never be to get it right 100% of the time because that's not possible. I would say that getting to the point of 90/10 is probably the most realistic top achievement for any of us beautifully imperfect humans, though 80/20 is probably more attainable for most. The great news is that the better we care for ourselves, the more we reflect, and the more we practice, the more we will naturally *"find the pause."*

JOURNAL PROMPT: GOAL SETTING

Take a moment to first write about the progress you've made thus far. Where were you with your anger a couple of weeks ago? Where were you with it a couple of months ago? And where are you now? Take a moment to celebrate your wins!

Next, write a detailed story of where you'd like to be with your anger six months from now. And then a year from now.

Next, list the steps you need to take to achieve those goals and the timeframe in which you can realistically take them. Example: "I need to reflect and journal five days a week and practice one self-regulation technique for five minutes, three times a week, for the next three weeks. And then I need to reassess my steps."

Lastly, write an intention to take those steps to the best of your ability in the timeframe you've laid out.

FIVE

REGULATION IN PRACTICE

Now that you're raising your awareness and have a toolbox full of regulation techniques that work for you, let's look at how this all comes together. Let's say your son does something to trigger you. In a split second, you feel your body react. Pressure builds in your chest, your heart rate increases, and your fists clench. You feel the desire to react behaviorally, yell, hit, or throw something. Before your unconscious mind (the amygdala) can take over, you invite your conscious mind (frontal lobes) to stay on scene. You focus on yourself, your needs, and your experience, setting aside the impulse to deal with your son's behavior. Congratulations, you've found the pause! But your blood is still boiling, and you must regulate before this glorious pause goes to waste. So, now what?

STEP 1: Mentally talk yourself through it.

Remember, an emotion's physiological experience lasts only 90 seconds, but our minds can keep that emotion active if we're not conscious of our mindset. So, we want to do our best to focus on ourselves and talk ourselves through the process of identifying our next steps.

"I'm triggered right now. What am I feeling? I'm angry. Okay. Why am I angry about this? Because that behavior made me feel unsafe. Okay. What do I need to stay regulated? I need to breathe and let out some sound in a healthy way. Do I need to step away from my child to do this? No, it's safe to do these things in front of him." [OR] "Yes. I need to step away. I don't want to scare him."

STEP 2: Take Action to Regulate

If you feel it's best to step away to be alone, and you can do so, here's how that might look: You'd ensure your son is in a safe space. You would get down on his level and let him know, as calmly as possible, that you need to step away to feel your feelings for a moment. This may upset him. That's okay. You must regulate yourself before you can help him regulate. An escalated adult *cannot* de-escalate an escalated child. Once you are regulated, you can return to him and help him regulate. You can then repair any ruptures caused by your need to step away and correct the original behavior that posed a challenge.

Whether you step away or not, and you've ensured that your son is safe, your focus is to stay on your feelings and needs for the time being. This is where you draw from the personalized toolbox you built in chapter 3 and use as many techniques as you need to regulate yourself.

STEP 3: Mentally check in with yourself

Before you return to your child or switch your focus back onto them, you want to ensure that you are regulated and capable of responding to their behavior or emotions respectfully, which aligns with your values as a mother.

Ask yourself:

"How am I feeling now?"

"Am I ready to respond to my child?"

"What is the best way to respond to my child in this situation?"

STEP 4: Shift your focus back onto your child

Now that you are regulated, you can respond to your child. Hold space for their big emotions. Connect with them once they're receptive to it. Help them regulate if they need to. Once you are both regulated and connected, you can respectfully correct their behavior if necessary.

WHEN DYSREGULATION CREEPS BACK IN

Sometimes we've taken all the right steps when we paused and regulated before responding to our child. But as we address the challenge with our child, we feel increasingly dysregulated again. Their screams or "defiant" behavior triggers us again, and we find ourselves back at square one. If this happens to you, start the process of regulating over again. It is okay to have to shift your focus to yourself again. If it helps to put earplugs in to drown out the triggering sounds of their cries, do that. If it helps to set aside correcting their behavior until later, do that. Remember, an escalated adult cannot de-escalate an escalated child.

SIX

CO-REGULATION

I couldn't write this book without speaking a bit about the important, often misunderstood topic of co-regulation. I think many parents feel like it's something that they have to learn to do for their children. But, co-regulation takes place anytime human beings of any age are in the presence of other human beings because our nervous systems naturally mirror those around us. Have you ever noticed how being around someone anxious, bummed out, or angry can influence you to start feeling the same way? Or when you witness someone get hit in the crotch, you naturally wince a little bit? This mirroring can even happen when we're watching a movie. When we watch a character fall to pieces in grief and become choked up or watch the two lovebirds reunite in the end, wrapped up in each other's arms, kissing passionately, we can't help but smile and feel their joy. This is a result of our brain's *mirror neurons*. These lovely little neurons activate when we perform and observe someone else performing the action. Our brain thinks we're experiencing the action by witnessing it.

Mirror neurons play a massive role in how children learn and form who they are. This is why our children always seem to be at their worst when we are extra tired or stressed out. They feel what we feel. They are mirroring us. Alternatively, when we can stay regulated through life's challenges, our children's nervous systems naturally follow suit.

In parenting, co-regulation refers to the caregiver being calm through their child's chaos. Depending on the situation, this can manifest in many ways, but the foundation is that the caregiver self-regulates. If you have found any degree of success in self-regulating through your journey through this book, you have also been co-regulating with your children. You're co-regulating each time they see you shake out your anger or breathe through your stress. Each time you rock your baby, you're co-regulating. You're co-regulating each time you sit calmly and hold space for your child while they cry. You're co-regulating when you validate your toddler's feelings during or after a tantrum. Each time you hug your child while they cry about their skinned knee or their first break up, you're co-regulating. And every time you coach your child through the very same regulation techniques you've learned in this book, you're co-regulating.

Powerful things are happening for your child on the inside, no matter how the process of co-regulation looks on the outside. It is through co-regulation that your child is learning how to do what you never learned as a child, to self-regulate. Each time you co-regulate with your child, their mirror neurons are activated to mirror your calm, and the more this happens, their brains become wired for more natural calm. Children raised with healthy co-regulation are more likely to grow into adults with more regulated default modes who are less easily triggered and have wider Windows of Tolerance.

Congratulations, Mama! Through your own experience of growth, you are breaking cycles for your children.

SEVEN

LIVING A FULL LIFE

I am confident that you have begun to see some serious transformations in your ability to regulate your emotions, but I must leave you with one last important point. The goal is not to avoid getting triggered by your children. Even if you have found yourself getting triggered less often, I promise you, you will get triggered again and again…and again…for the entirety of your life. You are human! Emotions are part of what makes us human. There is no shame in getting triggered or feeling angry. It's how you respond to those triggers and express those emotions that this book aims to shift in you. Remember that your triggers are gifts. They are messages from deep within that remind you that you have some wounds or unmet needs to address. They are an opportunity, a light being shed on the shadowy parts of your psyche where your wounds have been locked away. Using the somatic techniques you learned in this book, you have the power to free yourself from those wounds. With each trigger, ask yourself, "What can I learn from this anger right now?"

As I've said before, no matter how well-practiced you become, you will become overpowered by your emotions in some way again. You will make mistakes. You will still have days, weeks, or months where regulating yourself feels harder. Again, there is no shame in this. You are human. Humans get sick, tired, and stressed out; we grieve and navigate major life changes, new traumas, and all the many ups and downs life offers. And with those downs, our ability to stay regulated sometimes suffers. Living a full life means living through all the ups and downs and feeling the full range of emotions our incredible bodies and minds are gifted with. The beauty that life provides us is our ability to coregulate with our partners, friends, children, pets, and all those closest to us. We, humans, need one another. Lean on your loved ones when you need it. Allow others to help you. And if you find yourself at a point in this journey where you can't seem to stay on track on your own or even with the support of your loved ones, please reach out for help from a professional who can guide you through the healing work you may need.

Congratulations, Mama, you are no longer an "Angry Mom." You are now a "Regulated Mom." You are a beautifully imperfect, regulated mother.

ABOUT THE AUTHOR

Emilie Delworth lives in the Lake Tahoe area with her partner, Dave, and their daughter, Lucy. As a new mom, Emilie found herself drowning in dysregulation. Through her journey of healing from complex trauma and learning to regulate herself, Emilie grew passionate about helping other wounded mothers do the same.

Emilie is a Parenting Coach with a special focus on taking an intentional, trauma-informed approach to raising children based on the latest research on attachment theory, child development, and neuroscience. She is also an Addiction and Abuse Recovery Coach, specializing in helping women recover from all forms of wounding or trauma.

For more information about the services offered by Emilie, visit www.the-peaceful-mother.com.

SOURCES

ACA. *The Loving Parent Guidebook*.

Levine, Peter. *Healing Trauma*. Sounds True Audio.

"More on Hyper and Hypo-Arousal." *Trauma Thrivers*,
10 Mar. 2021,
https://traumathrivers.com/more-on-hyper-
and-hypo-arousal/.

Pedersen, Traci. "Amygdala Hijack: What It Is and
How to Prevent It." *Psych Central*, Psych Central, 14
Oct. 2021,
https://psychcentral.com/health/amygdala-
hijack#about-amygdala-hijack.

S, Pangambam. "Change Your Breath, Change Your
Life: Lucas Rockwood (Transcript)." *The Singju*

Post, 31 Mar. 2020,

https://singjupost.com/change-your-breath-change-your-life-lucas-rockwood-transcript/.

Segilia, Author Deana. "Harlow's Monkeys." *Exploring Experiments*, 3 Mar. 2016,

https://sites.psu.edu/dps16/2016/03/03/harlows-monkeys/.

"Therapy in a Nutshell." YouTube,

https://www.youtube.com/channel/UCpuqYFKLkcEryEieomiAv3Q.

"What Is the Window of Tolerance, and Why Is It so Important?" *Psychology Today*, Sussex Publishers,

https://www.psychologytoday.com/us/blog/making-the-whole-beautiful/202205/what-is-the-window-tolerance-and-why-is-it-so-important.

Cherry, Kendra. "What Is Attachment Theory?"

Verywell Mind, Verywell Mind, 16 Dec. 2022,

https://www.verywellmind.com/what-is-

attachment-theory-2795337.

Made in the USA
Las Vegas, NV
13 October 2023

79016136R00066